PRIVACY IN
THE DIGITAL AGE

THE
DARK WEB

BY SUE BRADFORD EDWARDS

CONTENT CONSULTANT
M. E. Kabay, PhD, CISSP-ISSMP
Professor of Computer Information Systems
Norwich University

Core Library

Cover image: The Dark Web is a part of the internet
where users can remain anonymous.

An Imprint of Abdo Publishing
abdobooks.com

abdocorelibrary.com

Published by Abdo Publishing, a division of ABDO, PO Box 398166,
Minneapolis, Minnesota 55439. Copyright © 2020 by Abdo Consulting
Group, Inc. International copyrights reserved in all countries. No part of this
book may be reproduced in any form without written permission from the
publisher. Core Library™ is a trademark and logo of Abdo Publishing.

Printed in the United States of America, North Mankato, Minnesota
022019
092019

Cover Photo: Sergey Nivens/Shutterstock Images
Interior Photos: Sergey Nivens/Shutterstock Images, 1; Shutterstock Images, 4–5, 8, 43;
Elise Amendola/AP Images, 10–11; Red Line Editorial, 14; Nadir Keklik/Shutterstock Images,
16–17; T. Lesia/Shutterstock Images, 20 (computers); Nasonov Vasiliy/Shutterstock Images, 20
(routers); Kyodo/AP Images, 22–23; STR/Reuters/Newscom, 26, 45; John Marshall Mantel/
Sipa USA/Newscom, 30–31; Aitor Serra Martin/Shutterstock Images, 35; Owen Humphreys/
PA Wire URN: 35947953/Press Association/AP Images, 36–37; Gene J. Puskar/AP Images, 39;
John Miller/AP Images, 41

Editor: Maddie Spalding
Series Designer: Megan Ellis

Library of Congress Control Number: 2018966002

Publisher's Cataloging-in-Publication Data

Names: Edwards, Sue Bradford, author.
Title: The dark web / by Sue Bradford Edwards
Description: Minneapolis, Minnesota: Abdo Publishing, 2020 | Series: Privacy in the digital age |
    Includes online resources and index.
Identifiers: ISBN 9781532118913 (lib. bdg.) | ISBN 9781532173097 (ebook) | ISBN
    9781644940822 (pbk.)
Subjects: LCSH: World Wide Web--Security measures--Juvenile literature. | Cybercrimes
    --Juvenile literature. | Computer systems--Protection--Juvenile literature. |
    Cybersecurity--Juvenile literature. | Privacy, Right of--United States--Juvenile
    literature.
Classification: DDC 005.8--dc23

CONTENTS

WHAT IS THE DARK WEB?

After school, Shon and Micah rode the bus back to their apartment building. Shon said, "I'm worried about the math test tomorrow. I need to get a good grade. Will you help me study?"

Micah said, "There are easier ways to get a good grade than studying. There's a site you can go to and a hacker will fix your grade. It's on the Dark Web. "

Shon crossed his arms. "Hackers sell people's credit card numbers on the Dark Web. I don't want to get mixed up in that."

The Dark Web is part of the internet.

Shon ran up the stairs toward his apartment. On the landing, he almost ran into his older brother. "What is the Dark Web?" he asked. "Micah said people can find hackers there. He said hackers can help fix people's test grades."

His brother frowned. "Hacking is against the law."

"I'm not going to cheat," Shon said. "Is the Dark Web all bad?"

"There's a lot of other stuff going on there, too," his brother explained. "Come on. I'll help you study."

PERSPECTIVES
A+ HACKING

Chris Roberts is a security expert. He works for Acalvio. This company detects and prevents online security problems. Among the problems it deals with are hackers attacking schools. On the Dark Web, parents and students can visit sites where they can hire hackers to change students' grades or attendance records. "When I was younger, I would have had to . . . break into the office physically to do this," Roberts said. "These days, the records are accessible online. The target is the same; however, the method has changed."

ANONYMITY

The Dark Web is part of the internet. On the Dark Web, people use chat rooms and websites. They can buy goods and services. They can communicate anonymously. This means that they can hide their names and personal information.

Anonymity makes the Dark Web attractive to criminals. People sell drugs, guns, and personal data over the Dark Web. Hackers also use the Dark Web. Students or parents can hire a hacker through the Dark Web. The hacker can break into a school computer and change a student's grade.

CRYPTOCURRENCY

Cryptocurrency is digital, computer-generated money. Computers transfer this money securely between users. Bitcoins, Litecoins, and Monero are types of cryptocurrency. They are traded online anonymously. When people pay for something on the Dark Web using cryptocurrency, the payment cannot be traced back to them.

Hackers break into computer systems.

But anonymity is not always bad. Some people want to remain anonymous because they feel threatened. They may live in places where it is against the law to speak out against the government. They may be jailed or hurt if they use their real names online. Some people use the Dark Web to share how the company they work for is breaking the law. They could lose their jobs if they used their real names.

Other people use the Dark Web to protect their personal information. Websites collect data on visitors. This data includes credit card numbers and other personal information. It can be stolen. People can be tracked. Some people use the Dark Web to keep this information private.

STRAIGHT TO THE
SOURCE

Eileen Ormsby is a journalist who has written books about the Dark Web. In a 2018 interview, she explained why some people use the Dark Web:

> *The Dark Web is a useful tool for people who need privacy and secrecy: people living under oppressive regimes may use it to share views that oppose their government, or even just to access Facebook. Journalists can use it to safely confer with their sources. . . .*
>
> *There are those who believe the Dark Web is the future of the internet and that . . . it will give us our privacy back. Our mobiles and PCs [personal computers] contain our entire life, information that is being heavily mined by everything from Facebook to the banks.*

Source: Greg Callaghan. "The Dark Web." *The Sydney Morning Herald*. The Sydney Morning Herald, March 9, 2018. Web. Accessed December 6, 2018.

Back It Up

The author of this passage is using evidence to support a point. Write a paragraph describing the point the author is making. Then write down two or three pieces of evidence the author uses to make the point.

CHAPTER
TWO

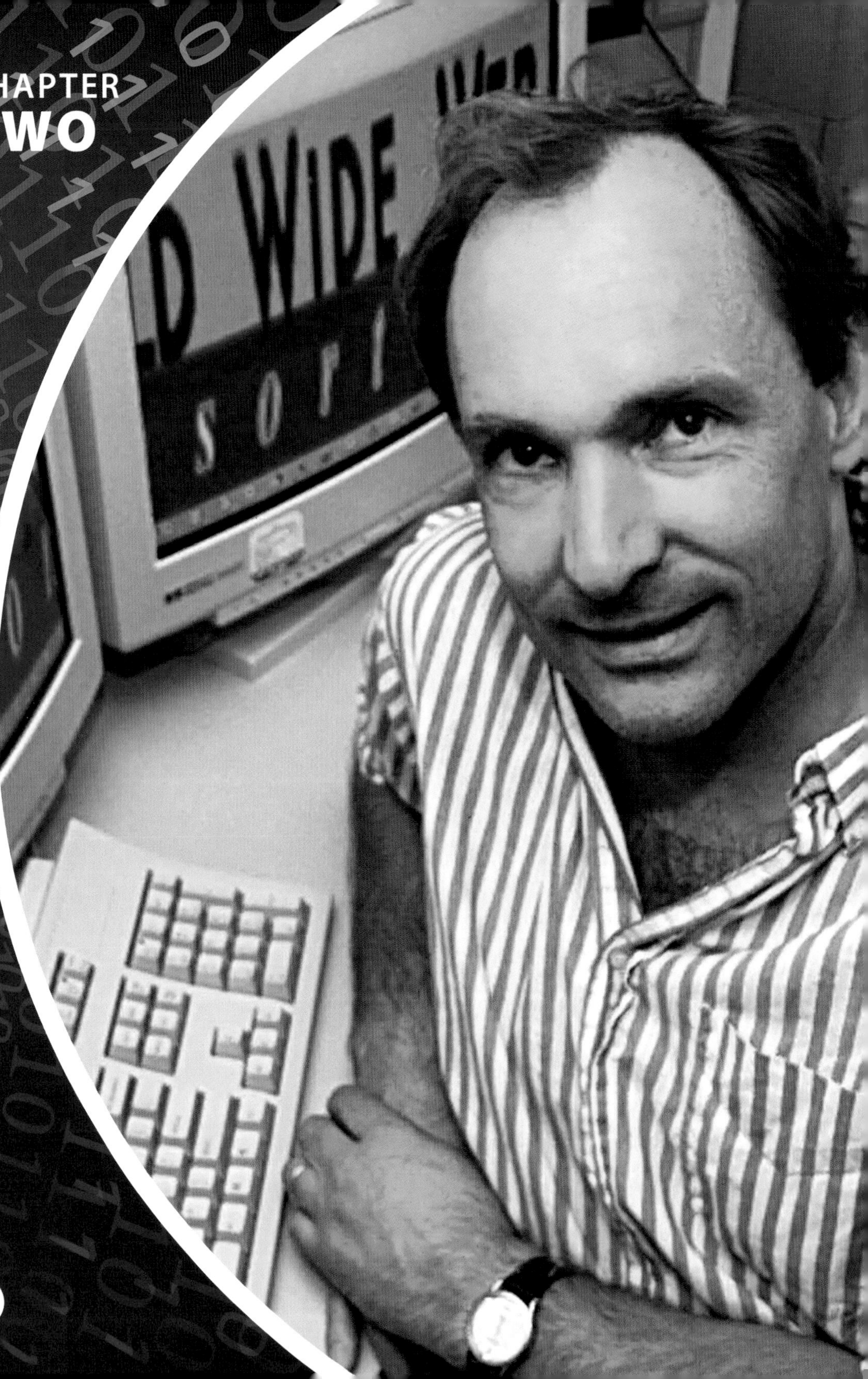

WEB LAYERS

The Dark Web is part of the internet. The internet is made up of networks, or groups of linked computers. These networks share information with each other. Millions of computers are connected through these networks.

The World Wide Web is the part of the internet that contains websites. The web is made up of different layers. The public part of the web is called the Surface Web. The Surface Web is made up of sites anyone can access to view and share information. YouTube is one example of a site on the Surface Web. The Surface Web can be accessed through a search engine, such as Google. People use

English scientist Tim Berners-Lee invented the World Wide Web in 1989.

PROTECTING COMPANIES FROM THREATS

Michael Marriot is a research analyst at a company called Digital Shadows. Digital Shadows helps protect other companies online. Digital Shadows explores the Dark Web to find information about companies that is exposed online. Hackers use this information to break into a company's computers. Analysts such as Marriot monitor online criminal forums to see what hackers are discussing and planning. They also use Google to search the Surface Web. A company's employee may accidentally post sensitive information or files there. Marriot said, "We want to [let] people know what's there and how that can expose them."

computer programs called web browsers to navigate the Surface Web. These browsers include Chrome, Edge, and Firefox.

THE DEEP WEB

The Deep Web is another part of the web. In many ways, the Deep Web is similar to the Surface Web. But Deep Web pages cannot be found through ordinary search engines. These sites often use security measures to protect information. People may have to enter a secret web address, username, or password to access a Deep Web site.

Deep Web sites often contain private information. For example, a person's social media profile may be visible only after the person enters a username and password. Someone searching the Surface Web cannot see it. It is on the Deep Web. Banks also use the Deep Web. Bank account information is stored in this part of the internet. When people check their bank accounts online, they are in the Deep Web. Email services, school grade websites, and online library catalogs also use the Deep Web.

HOW BIG IS THE DEEP WEB?

In September 2018, researchers at Internet Live Stats estimated the size of the Surface Web. They estimated that the Surface Web was made up of 1.9 billion sites. In 2012 the company BrightPlanet estimated that the Deep Web contained 4,000 to 5,000 times more sites than the Surface Web. BrightPlanet says that the number of Dark Web sites is changing too quickly to estimate the size of the Dark Web.

LAYERS OF THE INTERNET

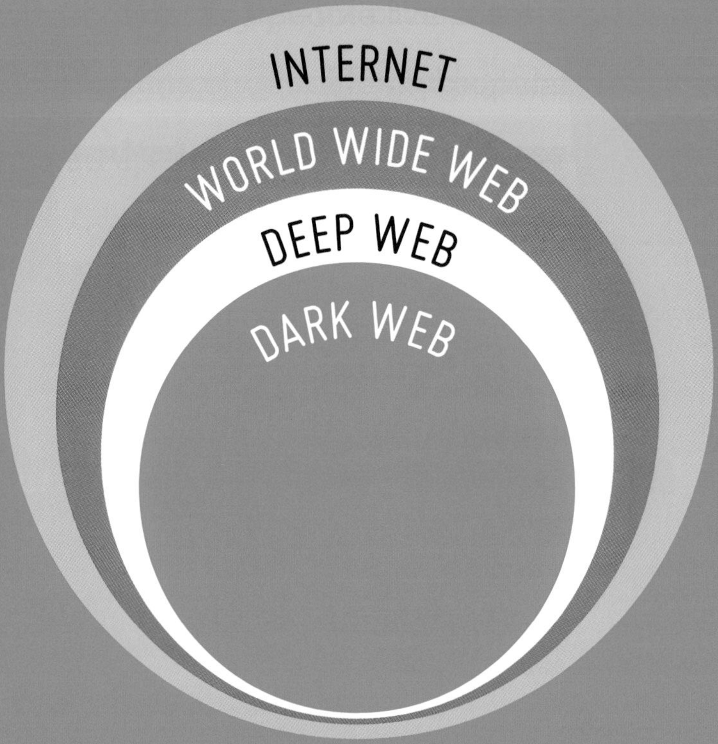

INTERNET

WORLD WIDE WEB

DEEP WEB

DARK WEB

The above diagram depicts the internet as layered networks. How does this diagram help you better understand the different parts of the internet?

THE DARK WEB

The least accessible part of the internet is the Dark Web, sometimes called the Darknet. The Dark Web lets users remain anonymous. A computer will not reveal any personal information while a user is on the Dark Web.

People need to use special software to access the Dark Web. This software includes programs such as Freenet, Invisible Internet Project (I2P), and the Onion Routing (Tor) project. These programs help hide users' locations and identities.

The Dark Web has a bad reputation. There is criminal activity on the Dark Web. But not everyone who uses it is a criminal. Some people simply want to live their lives without being watched.

FURTHER EVIDENCE

Chapter Two discusses different parts of the internet, including the Deep Web. What was one of the main points of this chapter? What evidence is included to support this point? Read the article at the website below. Does the information on the website support this point? Does it present new evidence?

EXPLORING THE DEEP WEB
abdocorelibrary.com/dark-web

CHAPTER
THREE

ACCESSING THE DARK WEB

Google and similar search engines cannot find Dark Web sites. This is because of how these search engines work. They use computer programs called crawlers to index sites. Crawlers gather information on websites. They also track where all the links on those websites go. Crawlers travel from link to link, gathering information as they go. They build up a list of all the known sites on the Surface Web. This list is what search engines use to find things online.

Dark Web sites are not linked to Surface Web sites. Crawlers cannot find and

The Dark Web cannot be found using ordinary search engines such as Google.

index them. Because of this, these sites do not show up in search results. The Dark Web is invisible to normal search engines. People who want to access the Dark Web need to use special software. Tor is one of the most popular programs used to navigate the Dark Web.

WEB ADDRESS SUFFIXES

The last several letters in a web address make up the suffix. The suffix is also called the top-level domain. The most common suffix is *.com*. The suffix *.edu* is used for schools and other educational organizations. The suffix *.gov* is used for government agencies. Sites on the Dark Web often use *.onion*. This shows that they are accessible through Tor.

THE ONION ROUTING PROJECT

In 2002 researchers at the US Naval Research Laboratory (NRL) created Tor. Tor is a type of software. It involves a process called onion routing. Routing is the process of sending data through a network of computers to reach a destination.

When a user visits a website, the data that makes up that site is routed through other computers on the way to the user's computer. In onion routing, data is sent through computers all over the world. This helps hide the identity of the original sender. The data also uses many layers of encryption. This keeps the data secret until it reaches its destination. People cannot read the data along the way. This encryption is what gives onion routing its name. Like an onion, it has many layers.

PERSPECTIVES
EXPLORING THE DARK WEB

Journalist Eileen Ormsby writes about the Dark Web. She has explored the Dark Web to better understand it. She discusses ways that people can access the Dark Web. But she warns people to be cautious. She says, "If you don't know someone in real life, you don't know them. Many people forget this and imagine themselves to be 'friends' with others because they chat online." People often share personal information with friends. Others can sell this information on the Dark Web.

HOW TOR
WORKS

Tor routes each request through at least three different computers. One computer encrypts the data and then sends it. The next computer decrypts, recrypts, and then sends the data. The below diagram shows how this process works. Does this diagram help you better understand the process? Why or why not?

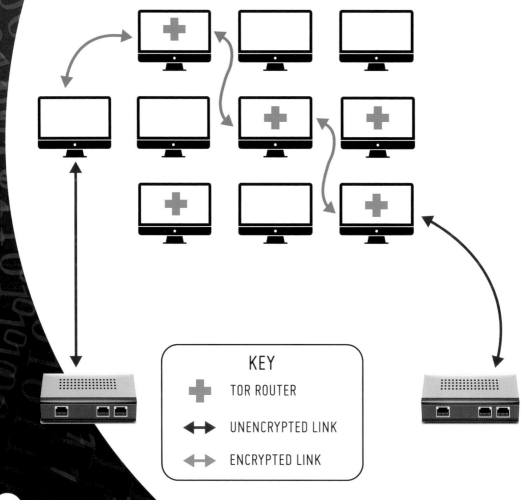

KEY

✚ TOR ROUTER

◄► UNENCRYPTED LINK

◄► ENCRYPTED LINK

Tor helps users remain anonymous, but it has its drawbacks. The process of passing data between computers, encrypting, and decrypting slows down access. Getting search results and linking to a site takes more time than when using the Surface Web. So does placing an order or posting on a forum. Users understand this is the price to be anonymous.

EXPLORE ONLINE

Chapter Three talks about Tor. The article at the website below goes into more depth on this topic. Does the article answer any of the questions you had about how Tor works?

TOR: OVERVIEW
abdocorelibrary.com/dark-web

CHAPTER FOUR

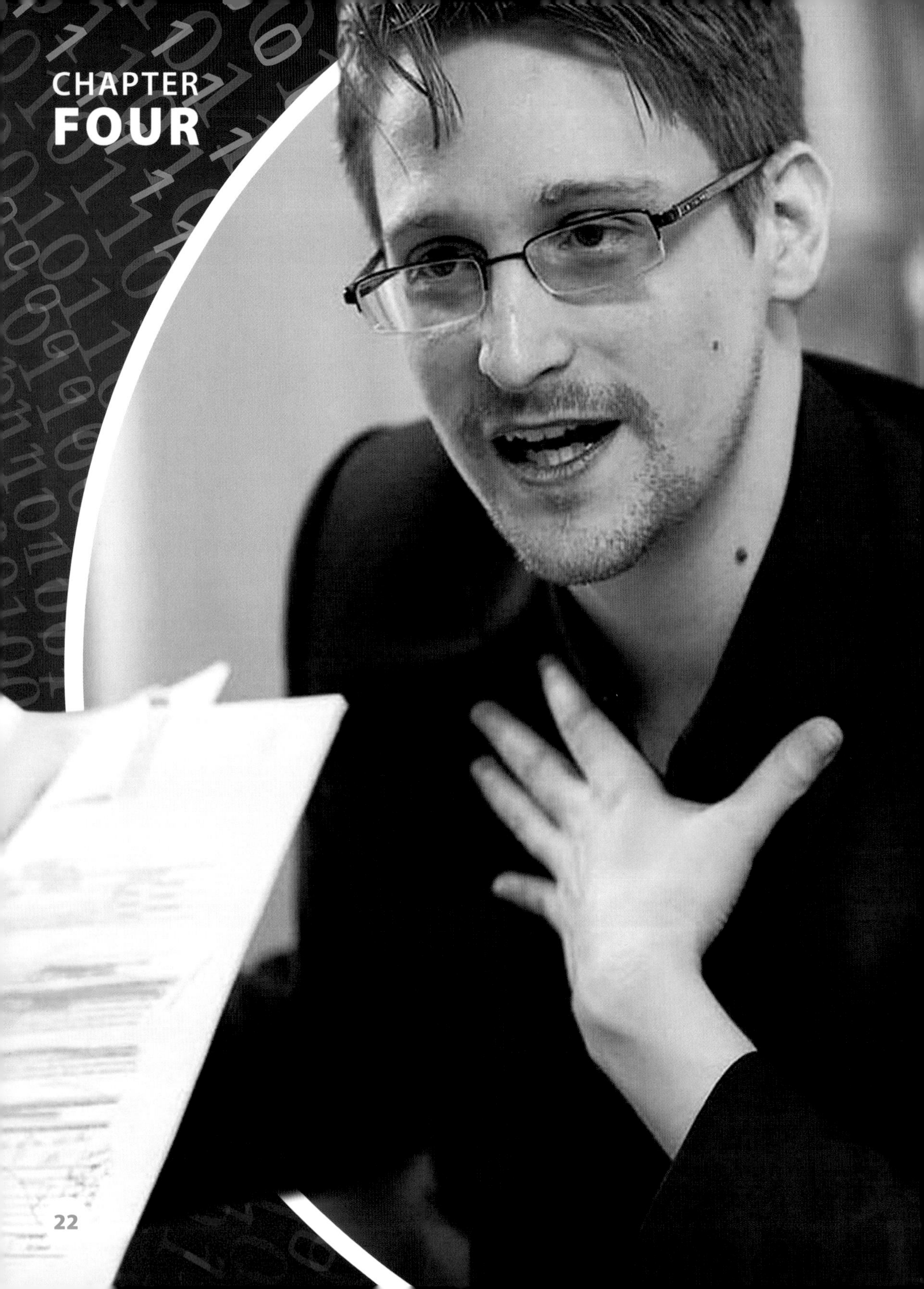

ANONYMOUS BUT NOT UNETHICAL

The name "Dark Web" may sound scary. But there are many reasons people may want to be anonymous. Not all of these reasons are criminal.

It is easy for computers to gather information from users. Browsers record credit card numbers when people buy things online. These programs also save a user's Internet Protocol (IP) address and the sites a user has visited. An IP address is a string of numbers and periods. Each device that goes online has

Edward Snowden used the Dark Web to find out more about how the US National Security Agency was spying on Americans.

AUTHOR JAMIE BARTLETT

Jamie Bartlett is the author of a book called *The Dark Net: Inside the Digital Underworld*. He explored the Dark Web while doing research for his book. He discovered that many Dark Web users wanted to have their story told. He says, "I think there is a very significant number of people who genuinely believe . . . that the internet in some ways was a great hope for libertarians." Libertarianism is a political belief. Libertarians believe that the government should have only limited control over people's lives and the economy. Bartlett says that these people use the Dark Web because they can communicate without government interference.

its own IP address. Web servers attach cookies. Cookies are text files that save information. They track the sites visited from an IP address. They collect data when people go online. Some cookies save passwords. Other cookies save details about the things people buy online. Cookies allow sites to use targeted advertising. Sites may suggest products that are similar to other products a person has bought. Information that is collected by cookies can be personal. A hacker could find and use this information.

Privacy also comes into play when people go online for help or information. The person may have a mental illness, such as depression. The person may be addicted to a drug or may be the victim of abuse. People who have these types of problems may be embarrassed about their situation. They want to talk to other people. But they may not want anyone to know who they are. The Dark Web can preserve their privacy.

USING THE DARK WEB FOR GOOD

Some governments limit the sites people can access. This is called internet censorship. Russia, Saudi Arabia, China, and Iran heavily monitor and censor sites. These countries block sites they consider immoral. They also block sites that disagree with the government. This limits the availability of information. People who live in these countries can use the Dark Web to access more news and information.

Some people in Iran publicly protest censorship, but others share their stories through the Dark Web for their safety.

The Dark Web can also be used to contact reporters. Some people may have information about crimes committed by a government. These crimes could include putting innocent people in prison or killing people who oppose the government. People who know about these crimes may want the public to know too. But they do not want their identities to be exposed. If that happens, the government may target them. The Dark Web has helped people in Iran and Egypt tell their stories.

Whistleblowers also may use the Dark Web. A whistleblower is someone who exposes the activities of an organization or a business. The activities might be illegal or unethical. Whistleblowers may give this information to reporters. The Dark Web helps protect a whistleblower's identity.

Edward Snowden is a well-known whistleblower. He worked for the US Central Intelligence Agency (CIA) and the US National Security Agency (NSA). The NSA gathers information on spies. The CIA gathers

EDWARD SNOWDEN

Edward Snowden is a computer programmer. He worked for the US National Security Agency (NSA). He collected classified documents. The documents showed that the NSA spied on US citizens. He gave these documents to the newspaper the *Guardian*. Snowden later allowed the *Guardian* to reveal his identity. The US government charged Snowden with being a spy. He fled the United States to escape these charges. Today, he lives in Russia.

information on other countries. Snowden used Tor to search the Dark Web for information. He showed reporters a top-secret NSA presentation. It was about how to use the Tor browser to reveal anonymous users' identities. Snowden showed reporters that the NSA was collecting information on many Americans. Since then, more information about the NSA has come out. The NSA collected records on most phone calls made in the United States. It also gained access to many people's Facebook posts, emails, and instant messages. It tracked the websites people had visited. Before Snowden's discovery, most people thought this information was private.

Some magazines and newspapers operate Dark Web sites. People can upload documents, photos, or recordings to these sites. SecureDrop is a Dark Web site operated by the *New Yorker* magazine. People can upload documents anonymously to the site. Then the magazine's reporters can make the information public.

STRAIGHT TO THE
SOURCE

Eric Jardine is an assistant professor of political science at Virginia Tech. He believes that certain sites on the Dark Web should be restricted. In a 2018 interview, he said:

> *People want solutions. They want to put a stop to them [crimes on the Dark Web], rightly so, and the problem is that there is an ability to minimize these negative abuses and, in discreet instances, stop them. So, you can take down specific markets . . . [but] a situation arises where one site shuts down and another site and set of vendors takes its place. You're not going to get rid of these technologies, but you can minimize the destruction that they cause.*

> Source: James Cullum. "#RealDeal Interview: Dealing with Dark Web Excesses Becoming 'Increasingly Important.'" *Homeland Security Today*. Homeland Security Today, May 22, 2018. Web. Accessed December 6, 2018.

Consider Your Audience

Adapt this passage for a different audience, such as your principal or friends. Write a blog post conveying this same information for the new audience. How does your post differ from the original text and why?

ILLEGAL ACTIVITY

Anonymity makes the Dark Web an attractive place for criminals. One example of this is the Silk Road. The Silk Road was an online marketplace. It was named after historic trade routes between eastern and western countries. People bought and sold illegal items on this Dark Web site. It was famous for its drug trade.

In 2011 an informant helped US officials find Ross Ulbricht. Ulbricht had created the Silk Road site. Many government agencies worked on the case. These agencies included the US Drug Enforcement Agency, the Federal

In January 2015, a few people gathered to protest at the trial of Ross Ulbricht, the founder of Dark Web site the Silk Road.

Bureau of Investigation (FBI), and the US Postal Inspection Service. Postal inspectors seized packages purchased through the Silk Road. Some of the packages contained drugs. Law enforcement officers arrested a seller in Australia. They seized drugs, weapons, and two telephones. These phones provided access to 20,000 messages. The messages created a digital trail. This trail showed the people Ulbricht had communicated with, when they had messaged, and the sites they had used. FBI agents took down the Silk Road site in September 2013. They later found and arrested Ulbricht.

Less than one month later, Silk Road 2.0 came online. The site's founder failed to remain anonymous. He used his own phone number to register the site. In late 2014, investigators shut down Silk Road 2.0.

DIRTY MONEY

The money a criminal earns by illegally selling an item or a service is called dirty money. Before the internet was created, a criminal had to launder dirty money. This meant spending it in a way that would not attract attention. Criminals set up fake businesses where they could spend the money. On the Dark Net, many criminals launder money by buying cryptocurrency, such as Bitcoins.

MONITORING THE DARK WEB

The anonymity the Dark Web provides is also attractive to terrorists. Anonymity hides terrorists' identities. This keeps them from being caught. They use the Dark Web to raise funds. They sell drugs. They also sell people into the sex trade.

Terrorists also use the Dark Web to ask for donations. Bitcoins and other cryptocurrencies are hard to trace. Because of this, terrorists ask their supporters to donate Bitcoins.

IDENTITY THEFT

Some people steal other people's personal information. Personal information can include a person's Social Security Number or credit card number. This information is part of a person's identity. Identity thieves can sell this information on Dark Web sites. Other identity thieves buy this information. They use this information to get money or other benefits. For example, an identity thief can use another person's credit card number to purchase things.

Identity thieves often use special software called malware to steal information. Malware can be purchased on the Dark Web. The thief installs the malware onto a store's computer system. Stores' computer systems often save customers' credit card information.

Ransomware is a common type of malware that hijacks a computer system until a person pays the hacker money.

The malware captures the credit card numbers. Then the identity thief can sell this information on the Dark Web. By selling this information to many people, the thief can make a lot of money.

Researchers wanted to know how often these sales were made. In 2015 a company called BitGlass created fake personal information. BitGlass planted the data on the Dark Web. The data was accessed 1,100 times in 12 days. This experiment helped prove that many identity thieves use the Dark Web. For this reason, some government agencies are working to make the Dark Web less anonymous.

CHAPTER
SIX

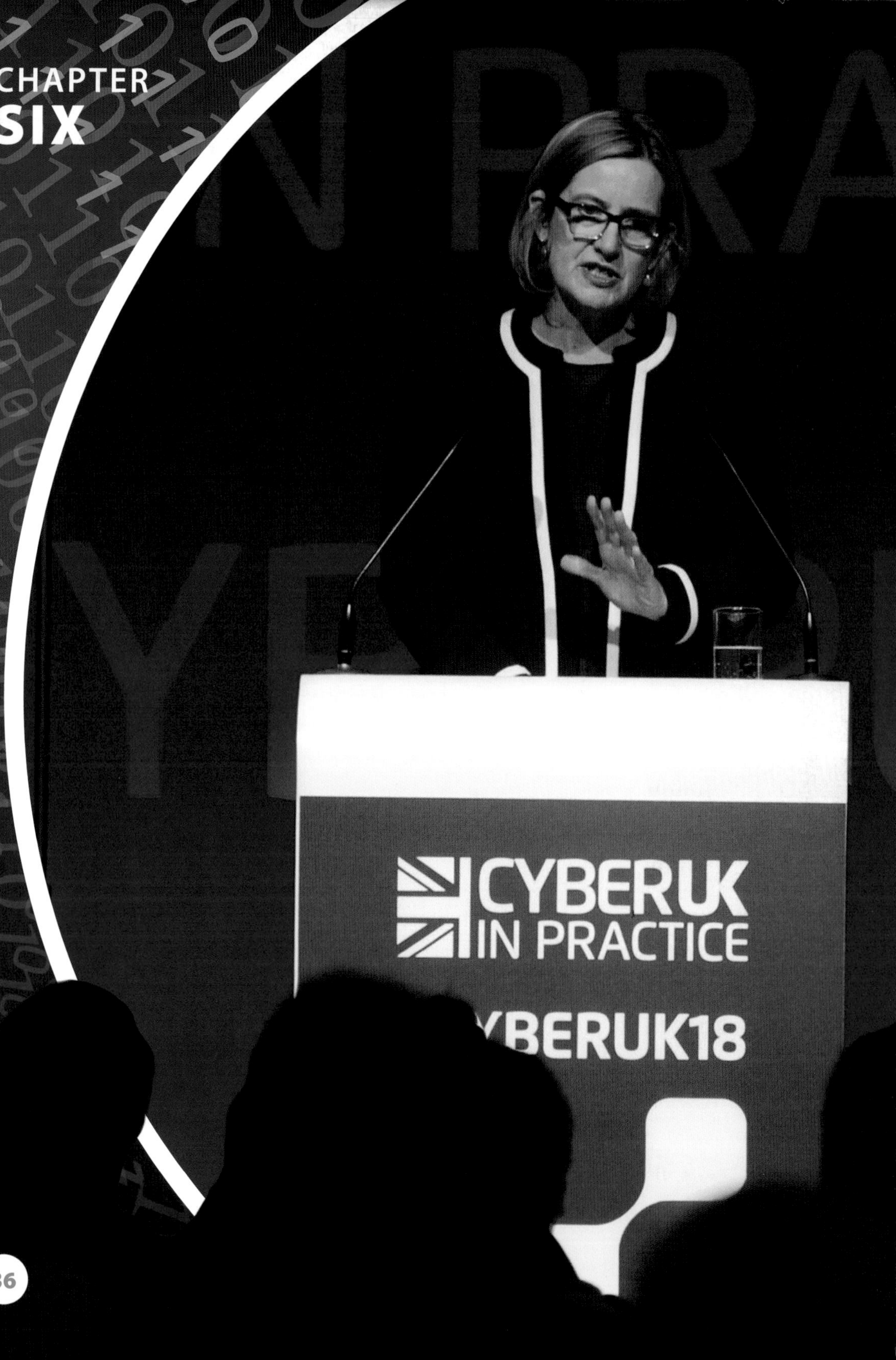

TRACKING DOWN CRIMINALS

Computer engineers are working on ways to fight Dark Web crimes. Researcher Chris White is working on a set of software tools called Memex. Memex can help investigators spot patterns. Finding patterns on the Dark Web can help law enforcement catch criminals. One of the Memex tools is Datawake. Datawake is used to search the Dark Web. It shows more than 25,000 hits from one search. Hits are websites that are found by a search. Datawake shows

At a 2018 cybersecurity conference, British politician Amber Rudd announced a plan to find criminals on the Dark Web.

the links between these hits. A link is a piece of information that appears on more than one site. It may be a person's phone number, name, or photo. Investigators can follow these leads to find criminals.

Tell Finder is another Memex tool. This program analyzes sites and advertisements on the Dark Web. It looks for common tells. A tell is something that accidentally communicates information. For example, some people change their expression every time they lie. A tell can also be a phone number or an email address. Sometimes a tell is a photo background. A wall color or painting

HONEYPOT TRAPS

FBI agents sometimes set up honeypot traps on the Dark Web. A honeypot trap is a site that claims to sell illegal items or promote illegal activities. The FBI defends the use of these sites. They say these traps lure criminals into giving themselves away. Other people think honeypot traps are unethical. They say that these traps encourage people to commit crimes. Today, hackers know how to identify and avoid many of these traps.

The FBI works to find and shut down illegal Dark Web sites.

can tell investigators where the photo was taken. When Tell Finder finds these tells, investigators know the sites or ads might be created by one anonymous criminal. This criminal uses the same locations, phone number, or email multiple times.

Tools such as these are making the Dark Web less anonymous to help take down criminals. Some people are critical of this. They want to keep the Dark Web anonymous. They believe this anonymity

HACKING MILITARY COMPUTERS

Andrei Barysevich is a senior threat researcher at Recorded Future. Recorded Future is a US cybersecurity company. It helps protect computer systems against attacks. Recorded Future discovered someone trying to sell information about a US Air Force drone on the Dark Web. A drone is an aircraft that flies without a pilot. The person selling the drone was a hacker. He had been exploring the internet. He hacked into an Air Force officer's computer and found files about the drone. Barysevich said this shows how vulnerable even military information can be.

is important. It protects whistleblowers and informants. It hides the identities of law enforcement officers as they work to trap criminals. It protects individual privacy. In these ways, Dark Web anonymity can benefit both law-abiding people and criminals. People can use the Dark Web to protect themselves or to commit crimes. Today, the debate about the Dark Web continues.

Hsinchun Chen, a professor at the University of Arizona, developed a tool that scans Dark Web sites to study terrorism.

FAST FACTS

- The World Wide Web is made up of three layers. The Surface Web is public. The Deep Web is protected by secret addresses or passwords. The Dark Web is even harder to access. People must use special software to access it.

- Tor is a popular software used to access the Dark Web. It helps users remain anonymous. The Tor browser sends requests through multiple computers. This makes them hard to trace.

- Many people want to remain anonymous online. Some do not want browsers and sites to store their personal information. Others use the Dark Web to share stories anonymously with a journalist. They do not want their identities known because a government or an organization might use this information to target them.

- Some criminals use the Dark Web to sell or buy illegal goods, such as drugs and guns. Some criminals sell personal information such as credit card numbers over the Dark Web.

- Law enforcement use software tools to find criminals on the Dark Web.

STOP AND
THINK

Surprise Me

Chapter Three talks about how people access the Dark Web. After reading this book, what two or three facts about the Dark Web did you find most surprising? Write a few sentences about each fact. Why did you find each fact surprising?

Take a Stand

Many people say that the Dark Web is a bad and dangerous place. Some people use the Dark Web to commit crimes. Other people use the Dark Web to protect their identities. Do you think anonymity makes the Dark Web dangerous? Why or why not?

You Are There

This book explores how journalists and activists can use the Dark Web. Imagine that you were a journalist using the Dark Web. Write a journal entry about why you chose to use the Dark Web. What are some benefits of using the Dark Web?

Another View

This book talks about the benefits and drawbacks of the
Dark Web. As you know, every source is different. Ask a
librarian to help you find another source about this topic.
Write a short essay comparing and contrasting the new
source's point of view with that of this book's author.
What is the point of view of each author? How are
they similar and why? How are they different
and why?

GLOSSARY

censorship
the process of suppressing or removing text that is considered offensive

cryptocurrency
digital currency or money

encryption
the act of coding data so that it cannot be understood in order to keep it private

forum
a part of the internet where people have an online discussion

hacker
someone who breaks into computer systems

identity
the factors that make up who a person is

informant
a person who shares information about secret or criminal activities

server
a computer in a network that shares files with other computers in the network

terrorism
the act of using violence or threats to frighten people

whistleblower
someone who reveals a business's or organization's illegal or unethical activities

ONLINE
RESOURCES

To learn more about the Dark Web, visit our free resource websites below.

Core Library
CONNECTION
FREE! COMMON CORE MULTIMEDIA RESOURCES

Visit **abdocorelibrary.com** or scan this QR code for free Common Core resources for teachers and students, including vetted activities, multimedia, and booklinks, for deeper subject comprehension.

Booklinks
NONFICTION NETWORK
FREE! ONLINE NONFICTION RESOURCES

Visit **abdobooklinks.com** or scan this QR code for free additional online weblinks for further learning. These links are routinely monitored and updated to provide the most current information available.

LEARN
MORE

Hudak, Heather C. *Helpful Hackers*. Minneapolis, MN: Abdo Publishing, 2018.

Smibert, Angie. *Inside Computers*. Minneapolis, MN: Abdo Publishing, 2019.

INDEX

About the Author

Sue Bradford Edwards is a Missouri nonfiction author who writes about science, culture, and history. Her other books include *Women in Science* as well as two books cowritten with Duchess Harris, *Hidden Human Computers: The Black Women of NASA* and *Black Lives Matter*.